Rose

Spiders

Illustrated by David Wright

OXFORD
UNIVERSITY PRESS

OXFORD
UNIVERSITY PRESS

Great Clarendon Street, Oxford OX2 6DP

Oxford University Press is a department of the University of Oxford.
It furthers the University's objective of excellence in research, scholarship,
and education by publishing worldwide in

Oxford New York

Athens Auckland Bangkok Bogotá Buenos Aires Calcutta
Cape Town Chennai Dar es Salaam Delhi Florence Hong Kong Istanbul
Karachi Kuala Lumpur Madrid Melbourne Mexico City Mumbai
Nairobi Paris São Paulo Shanghai Singapore Taipei Tokyo Toronto Warsaw

with associated companies in Berlin Ibadan

Oxford is a registered trade mark of Oxford University Press
in the UK and in certain other countries

British Library Cataloguing in Publication Data available

Hardback ISBN 0-19-910688-6
Paperback ISBN 0-19-910689-4

1 3 5 7 9 10 8 6 4 2

Printed in Spain

Contents

▶ The hunters 4

▶ The trappers 6

▶ The web-builders 8

▶ All sorts of webs 12

▶ Making spiderlings 14

▶ Supermums 16

▶ Leaving home 18

▶ All over the world 21

▶ A closer look at spiders 24

▶ Scared of spiders? 26

▶ Spiders for supper 28

▶ Glossary 30

▶ The hunters

Suddenly the spider is there.
It comes from nowhere, creeping
like a cat, without a sound.
Then – the spider jumps!

It holds the fly with its legs and
stabs with its fangs. The venom
works quickly.

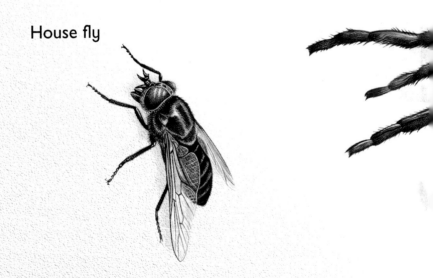

House fly

The fly stops struggling; it is paralysed. Now it is ready to eat, the spider sucks it dry.

The jumping spider doesn't make a web. With eight good eyes and eight strong legs, the jumping spider is a great hunter.

Jumping spider
Salticus scenicus

▶ The trappers

In the dead of night a beetle walks the forest floor. The trapdoor spider hides in its burrow. It knows the beetle is coming.

Around the burrow are silk trip lines. The spider feels the lines vibrate. The beetle comes closer… and closer.

Trapdoor spider
Liphistius desultor

Pop! The trapdoor opens.

Out darts the spider. It grabs the beetle and pulls it underground.

Pop! The lid closes.

Trapdoor spiders don't need good eyesight. They can feel their prey coming. Trapdoor spiders are great hunters too. They don't make webs either.

The web-builders

All spiders make silk but only a half of all spiders make webs.

The best-known web is the orb web. In any garden you will find dozens of orb webs or a garden spider busy making one.

First the spider makes a silk thread. She draws it out of her spinnerets like liquid silk, but it soon hardens.

Then she begins to build.

Garden spider
Araneus diadematus

legs

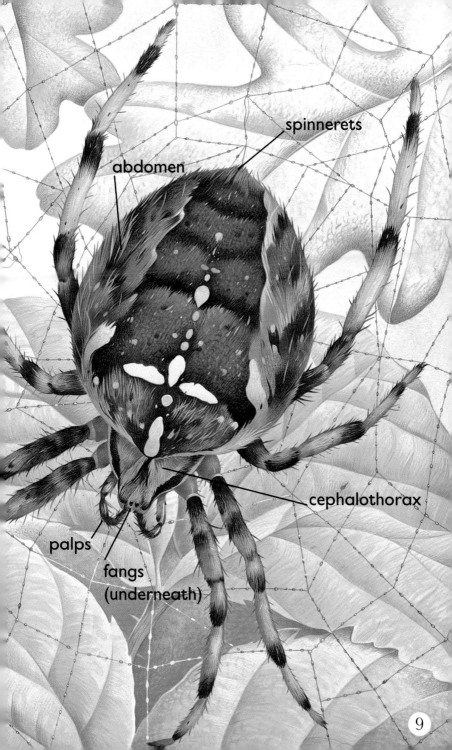

spinnerets

abdomen

cephalothorax

palps

fangs
(underneath)

9

The spider fixes one end of the thread to a branch. The wind carries her to another nearby. Now she has a bridge.

She crawls back along it with a second thread, then drops down. Now she has a Y shape.

Back and forth she travels from the centre making spokes, like a wheel.

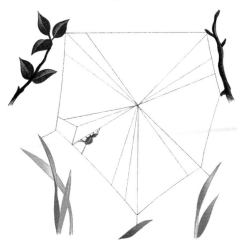

She joins them up in a spiral pattern. In one hour she will have a perfect web ready to catch her prey.

▶ All sorts of webs

There are many different kinds of web. The hammock web spider hangs beneath her web, waiting for the insect to fall in.

Hammock web spider
Linyphia triangularis

Sheet webs have a funnel where the spider hides. Above there's a tangle of sticky threads ready to catch the insect.

Then the spider rushes out… and grabs it!

sheet web with
Tegenaria domestica

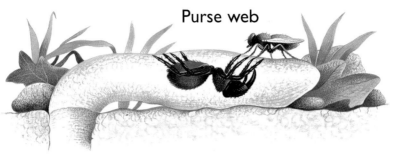
Purse web

Purse web spiders hide inside a silk tube, waiting for the insect to walk across it. Then she grabs it!

Purse web spider
Atypus affinis

Most webs are made by female spiders. Female spiders are bigger than males, sometimes twenty times bigger! So the male has to be very careful when he comes to mate. He might get eaten by mistake!

▶ Making spiderlings

The male garden
spider fixes a thread
to the female's web.
He pulls it gently,
like ringing
a doorbell.

Garden spider
*Araneus
diadematus*

When the male wolf spider meets a
female, he waves his legs in the air.

Wolf spider
*Pardosa
amentata*

The male jumping spider does a little sideways dance.

Jumping spider
Salticus scenicus

The male nursery web spider brings a gift, perhaps a tasty fly wrapped in silk.

But sometimes, if the female is hungry, the male still gets eaten!

Nursery web spider
Pisaura mirabilis

▶ Supermums

Spiders make very good mothers. The female lays her eggs in an egg sac wrapped in a silk cocoon.

a spider's egg sac

The nursery web spider spins a silk tent. Her babies live inside the little nursery until they're big enough to leave and find food for themselves.

Nursery web spider's tent
Pisaura mirabilis

Wolf spider and her babies
Pardosa amentata

The wolf spider is a supermum!
She carries her egg sac with her,
stuck to her spinnerets. When the
eggs hatch out she carries her babies
on her back too.

► Leaving home

Some spiders only lay two eggs at a time; some garden spiders lay a thousand. In spring the eggs begin to hatch. There are so many the spiderlings may soon start to eat each other. If they want to survive they must escape.

They spin their first silk threads and the wind carries them like little parachutes. A thousand eggs may hatch but soon many babies will be eaten.

Did you know...
some Nephila spiders can produce 1000 eggs in ten minutes?

Lizards, birds, frogs, toads and shrews, even some insects like wasps and beetles, eat spiders. But enough spiders survive. It is thought that on a summer's day there may be two million in a field of grass.

All over the world

Wherever you go in the world you will find spiders: in jungles, swamps, deserts, beaches, deep caves and coal mines, on top of mountains, under Arctic snow.

Some spiders even live in lakes and ponds. The swamp spider is so light it can walk on water. It sits on a leaf dangling its feet, fishing for insects or tadpoles.

Swamp spider
Dolomedes fimbriatus

Water spider
Argyroneta
aquatica

The water spider spins a silk web
under the water. It ties it to a plant
and fills it with a bubble of air.
It lives inside its underwater web,
swimming out to catch food, like
tadpoles and water insects.

A closer look at spiders

Insect

Spider

Spiders aren't insects. Spiders belong to the arachnid family. Insects have six legs and three parts to their bodies. Spiders have eight legs and two parts. They also have two fangs which they use to bite their prey and inject them with venom.

Most are small and hunt insects. Some are so small you'd need a magnifying glass to see them.

Tiny house spider *Oonops domesticus*

Some spiders are so big they'd cover a dinner plate. The bigger ones can eat mice, birds, frogs, even lizards and snakes. But spiders hardly ever bite people.

Mexican red knee tarantula
Brachypelma smithi

▶ Scared of spiders?

In fact, spiders help humans by
eating pests that carry germs and
disease. Yet many people are afraid
of spiders. Why is that? Is it
because they move quickly?
Is it because they appear
without a sound?
Is it because they
have so many
long hairy legs?

Mexican blond tarantula
Aphonopelma chalcodes

Black Widow spider
Latrodectus mactans

Australian Funnel
web spider
Atrax robustus

We call all large hairy spiders tarantulas. Most people are afraid of tarantulas but even their bite doesn't often kill. The Black Widow spider can kill. So can the Australian Funnel web spider.

But most spiders are harmless. They only hunt for food to stay alive. Sometimes spiders are hunted too.

Spiders for supper

The Piaroa Indians hunt the giant tarantula. They coax it out of its hole. Then they pounce! They hold it with their thumbs. They stab it with a wooden spike. The spider stops struggling. It is dead.

The Indians wrap it in
leaves, like a parcel, all
wrapped up and ready
to cook. They cook the
spider in a fire. They
think it is delicious.
The Piaroa Indian hunts
for his food. Just like the
spider. They are both
great hunters.

Giant tarantula
Theraphosa blondi

29

▶ Glossary

This glossary will help you to understand what some important words mean. You can find them in this book by using the page numbers given below.

There are over 30000 different kinds of spider. Very few have common names, but every single species has a scientific name which is written in Latin like this: *Araneus diadematus.*

 abdomen The abdomen of a spider is the main part of its body. **9**

 cephalothorax The head and the part joining the head to the abdomen of a spider. **9**

 cocoon A cocoon is a silk case the spider wraps her egg sac in to protect it. **16**

 egg sac An egg sac is a silk bag in which the spider keeps her eggs. **16, 17**

fangs Fangs are the sharp claws on the spider's head which it uses to bite its prey and poison it. **4, 9, 24**

 mate When a male and female spider join up to make babies, it is called mating. **13**

 palps Palps are feelers which a spider uses to touch and test things when looking for food. **9**

 prey An animal that is hunted by another animal for food is called its prey. **7, 11, 24**

 spiderlings Spiderlings are baby spiders. **14, 18**

 spinnerets The openings at the tip of a spider's abdomen from which it draws out silk. **8, 9, 17**

Reading Together

Oxford Reds have been written by leading children's authors who have a passion for particular non-fiction subjects. So as well as up-to-date information, fascinating facts and stunning pictures, these books provide powerful writing which draws the reader into the text.

Oxford Reds are written in simple language, checked by educational advisors. There is plenty of repetition of words and phrases, and all technical words are explained. They are an ideal vehicle for helping your child develop a love of reading – by building fluency, confidence and enjoyment.

You can help your child by reading the first few pages out loud, then encourage him or her to continue alone. You could share the reading by taking turns to read a page or two. Or you could read the whole book aloud, so your child knows it well before tackling it alone.

Oxford Reds will help your child develop a love of reading and a lasting curiosity about the world we live in.

Sue Palmer
Writer and Literacy Consultant